Kathy
xx

EARTH ANGELS

poetry & prose
Melissa M. Combs

"Therefore do not cast away your confidence,
which has great reward. For you have need of endurance,
so that after you have done the will of God,
you may receive the promise."
- Hebrews 10:35

EARTH ANGELS

poetry & prose
MELISSA M. COMBS

THE TRUTH IS, NOTHING WAS
EVER GOING TO STOP YOU FROM

rising.

like the wind of a thousand hurricanes,
or like the flames of a forrest fire blazing
rapidly out of control,

a woman with a burning desire
stops for *nothing* and for *no one*.
once she has set her sight on what it is
that she truly wants,
soon after, *it is hers for the taking.*

let me not mistake the venom
being sucked out of my soul
as blood being drained from my body...
and let me not be so frail
as to crumble,
bow to, or curse my pain.

for soon, i am to become the healer,
the risen, and the way.

EARTH ANGELS

little girl,
look up.
jump out
of your body
and into your
real one.

there is a universe
that runs vast and deep.

you are that universe —
larger than your body,
and more than
your skin and bones.

funny thing about growth —
sometimes the expansion feels as though
your soul is ripping at the seams.

and then it was revealed to us,
that all along, we were the *a n g e l s* —

both the righteous and the fallen,

tirelessly at war with one another,
and ultimately with ourselves.

one day
you will channel
all of this pain,
transform it into *art*,
and set fire to the
world.

only those threatened by you
will ever tell you that you are 'too much.'
'too much woman' or 'too much wild.'

but the truth is,
they're simply scared they'll never
measure up.

if anything,
thank them for leaving
you there to drown.

they awakened in you
a soul brave enough to
swim the depths
that once
you had only
ever dreamt of.

you don't need a man right now.

what you need is to strip down naked
for the first time in your life
and lie underneath a full moon;
you need a shot or two of
tennessee whiskey,
an ocean to bathe in,
a blank canvas to paint on,
and a mirror to finally show you
your self worth.

you may need many things right now...
but a man is *not* one of them.

before you are given wings,
you are given trials.

so if ever you feel as though it is the end…
in reality, it is only one of your endless
new beginnings.

ever notice that people aren't
making their wishes on idle stars,
but on the one's that are willing
to *aim, shoot,*
and even *fall?*

it's a wicked world, my love,
but still you must dance…

for with every step that you take,
a thousand serpents must die,
and with every graceful movement
made,
another parsec of air is to be
owned by you.

this world is yours,
all yours.

you must never stop dancing.

your dreams are more than
dreams, they are *prophecy.*

and you are more than skin
and bones,
you are *eternity.*

she was the rays of a thousand suns,

craved by the men of very dark worlds.

do not be so quick to paint yourself
black for any man — *even him.*
remember,
he wants what you have,
not what he already is.

know your worth and
help him instead to reach
for his light.

EARTH ANGELS

one day you will look into
the mirror and realize
that the version standing
before you is the very version
that you once dreamt up in
your head.

you'll realize that you have
arrived.
you have finally arrived.

and from there on out,
everything that you do
will be done from love,
not from lack.

if the trees exist
amongst the wild flowers,
neither asking one another
to change,
and if the shoreline welcomes
the waves
as they are,
often times violent and
unpredictable...

then surely, wild woman,
you deserve the very same —
a love so pure
that it would die at the thought
of ever asking you
to change.

and some days
you just have to be thankful
that the sun still rises for you…
and more importantly,
that the moon still trades places
to give you necessary rest.

those are the days you learn
that even when others forsake you,
the universe never has nor ever
will.

if they are not comfortable
with your wild,

by all means, *let them go.*

but don't you dare allow them
the power as to why you
cease to grow.

women like her have
this innate wolf-like spirit
inside of them…

always hungry for more
of life,
but never starved.

i looked into his eyes and said,
"for you, i'd risk the fall."

he said,
"i would never dream of letting you fall...
just promise me instead, that all costs,
you will rise."

you've spent your entire life
longing to be a rose. *why?*

to be ripped from your soil,
admired for a day or two
and then left for dead?
is that really the life that you desire?

remain the wildflower.
remind everyone
that there are some flowers that
are meant to grow chaotically
free.

i happen to favor
expectations...

they push us beyond the
excuses that we have for so
long allowed to erode us
from the inside out.

expectations
i like to imagine as vicious wolves,
chasing us.

in our weakness,
we imagine them catching up
to us; devouring us.
we, without much control,
see ourselves being ripped to
shreds by teeth.

but what happens when we take
a leap of faith, standing still
amongst the wolves,
refusing to run?

how might we react then
to discover that *we are the wolves?*
strong enough to meet and even
exceed expectations;
resilient enough to have
more placed among our path.

EARTH ANGELS

just when you feel
as though you are dying,
you will *transform*
into a new
creation —
beautiful beyond your
wildest dreams.

the goal is to rise up so high
that you could never again reach me —
so high that the sound of your name
could never again shake me,
or send me crashing
breathless to my knees.

so high that i may never
again be broken by the false
hopes of a forever, you and i.

so high
in fact
that i may barely remember there
ever existed a 'you and i.'

i am both the risen
and the fallen;

the fire and the water
needed to extinguish
the flames;

weakness and power;

destructive winds
and cleansing rains;

a child born of
romance between
the angels and the
demons;

a spiritual gymnast,
perfecting the art of balance,
to end the war,
once and for all.

a master alchemist;
human.

caught somewhere in between
human and celestial —
that is an earth angel.

human —
vomiting words; creating art,
just because, well… we can.

celestial —
retracting and reshaping our words
because we know that they are more
than just words.

mutants, with a gift and a curse.

well, here i go again,
shapeshifting.
i'm going to stop spilling my every
thought now,
like the way you left me lost at s —

stop. retract. reshape.

too many
desire to fit in,
forgetting that it
is the highest honor
to be the *one in billions*,
standing out.

i guess i had gotten so used
to turning words into staircases
to climb my way out of the pain,
that i had forgotten that it is
okay to feel...
and that there is an incomparable
beauty to vulnerability.

looking back
i have always had a way
of chasing the facade
of perfectionism —
so subtle that it goes
unnoticed for far too long;
so subtle that my DNA
code glitches and confuses
me with machine;
so subtle that i lose myself
in an identity that is anything
but me.

but this right here
this is me...

so when you ask me if
i am whole,
the truth is,
i don't really know.

on a monday i am convinced
that i am,
yet on wednesday, i feel anything
but.

and if this is not for you;
if i am not for you...
then you are under no
obligation to stay.

but this is me...
and i am learning to be okay
with not fully being okay.

one thing i can tell you
about the journey
is that is filled with an immense
amount of both beauty and pain.

and i can't be certain just yet,
but if i had to guess,
i'd say that those that learn
to focus intently on the beauty,
will soon know very little of the pain.

it's not mania.
it's an open door
into another world —
airwaves
intertwining and dancing
with the
airwaves of
the one that we are in;
a glimpse into the future;
a taste of the truth.

it's not depression.
it's the settling back
into earth
once the door to the other
world closes,
as you are left to fulfill
your destiny.

the in between
is a vicious wind storm,
but you my love
were designed to
catch hold of and control
the storm.

there is rest on the
other side of awakening —

bliss;
euphoria;
access to the world that
you have always dreamt of.

but hasn't waking up
always been the hardest part?

from the ashes
the rise of the
phoenix takes place,
a beautiful and majestic
legend…

and legends my dear,
legends never die.

imagine where we would
be if we could learn to
listen rather than accuse;
to extend empathy,
rather than judge;
and to love thy neighbor
as our own body, mind, and soul;
where we would be
once we learn that no hand
is clean,
yet all worthy of being washed
cleaned.

whatever you do,
you must promise yourself
to always keep a hold on
wonder and refuse to let
it out of reach.

for if you have wonder,
then you too have hope.
and if you have hope,
it is notorious for growing into
faith…
and if you have faith,
then it will lead you to love.

and if you have love…
then you, my dear, you have it all.

EARTH ANGELS

i learned that i was as angelic
as i had always hoped to be,
the day that i chose to
wish you and her happiness;
to wish you a life filled
with love...
if even not with me.

not all rules were meant to be followed.

there will be some things, people, and
circumstances that are worth going against
the grain and walking the line for.

love should always be one of those things,
and yourself, one of those people...
under *any* and *all* circumstances.

i'll admit that i have always
had a way with enlarging
and assigning far too much
power to the way that the
cards have been stacked against me,
and far too little
to the miracles loudly
stirring within me.

but here i am,
once and for all,
shifting…
from the receiver to
the creator,
i am born.

therefore, the moment that you pick up your own pen,
you are a new creation; old weaknesses have
passed away…

behold, a new and powerful creation
has come into being.

by now it should be no secret
that humans will fail you, and often,
at that —
their lights flickering on and off;
such flawed creations.

but tell me,
when have the stars ever
refused their positions in the sky for you?
have they ever failed you, if even once,
when you were in need of
a light to guide your steps?

maybe in the times that others fail you
the universe is simply begging of you
to call out,
and reconnect.

EARTH ANGELS

so they didn't see you for
who you really were…
can you blame them?

an angel of the earth,
disguised in the flesh of a human.

life gets easier when you make peace with this —
that very few
you will meet in this
lifetime will have been trained in discernment,
and cloaked in wisdom.

only the one's that are
meant to see you will ever truly see you.
and i promise you this,
the depth in which they see you will
long make up for the lack of vision in
the others.

EARTH ANGELS

if you had never broken my heart,
who would i be?

honestly, if i had to guess,
i'd be a fraud, only half alive;
an ego alcoholic drunk in false power.

and as absurd as it may sound,
the answer to every equation —
less than.

i know that this is not the answer
expected of me...
but the truth is,
to feel your love and then to lose it
was a death and a rebirth all in one...

and what was reborn in me
i happen to favor far more than what
once lived.

EARTH ANGELS

you love like you were built to withstand
a thousand fiery deaths.

you forgive as though it were as natural as
breathing, though you have never been
formally taught to.

you pick up the heaviest shards of your soul
and you sculpt them into something light
and beautiful.

and still you buy into the lie that
you are not enough?

the same people that judge your steps
would tremble if they had to step so much
as an inch in your shoes…

keep walking the narrow path.

i promised you that i would stay
through it all —
purposely and meticulously pricked
my flesh with thorns,
held my heart over the flames,
and fought my best, for years,
to weather the storm.

but tell me, what would be left of me
should i continue pressing on?

therefore, if you and i are meant be,
i pray on that day that you find once and
for all, a whole and
healthy version of me.

EARTH ANGELS

"if you could travel back in time and speak
to a lost loved one,
who would you choose?"

myself. *a*nd i'd tell that tragically sad,
yet beautiful young girl,
that she was wasting her time,
and more importantly,
the best years of herself,
desiring to be picked by hands
that she would,
in time,
find to be unworthy.

so let them leave…
in fact this time help them to pack their bags.

and even if you have to choke back on tears
as you do so,
do not let that stop you from reaching for
the next item needed.

you see, women like you were never meant
to chase but to effortlessly upgrade and replace.

we all at some point or another
are touched by the very same flames...
the only difference really is what we allow
the flames to make of us.

sadly some will fall
like ashes, and ashes they are
to remain.
others refine effortlessly as silver....
and the rest fight a grueling battle to
reform themselves from the ashes they
wished never to become.

and while i used to envy those that were
so easily refined,
i have since then grown a healthier respect
for those that fight to reform from their ashes.

they are the one percent;
the anomalies.

you deserve universes…
but so do they.

so if i could press upon you just one simple principle,
it would be to love them the way that you too desire
to be loved.

you mean to tell me that she faced
it all while trembling,
yet still she persevered?

though i wanted reciprocated love,
it was in the unreciprocated
that i found my strength.

there i found myself
staring at the pain that i
had once feared.

befriending it i said,
"you may live inside of me under
two conditions:
one, you must allow me to learn from
you; teach me everything that you know…
and two, you must always leave room
inside of me for the purest of love to grow."

CARTH ANGELS

pay close attention to what is actually sent to harm you,
and what simply is working in the shadows to strengthen you.
what feels like a curse today
may in fact reveal itself as a blessing tomorrow...

so in the meantime, make what you can of the pain
and always — *always* hold tightly to your faith.

EARTH ANGELS

they thought that their
lies would destroy you
and turn you into a monster...

but look at you,
you've gained *a n g e l* wings
instead.

i no longer fear pain.

you see
pain
strengthens,
while comfort gives birth
to complacency
and slowly kills...

and damn it,
i am so tired of living this life dead.

EARTH ANGELS

i am no longer a victim
dying over our separation,
but a warrior embracing
her transformation.

darling,
you did not withstand
that agonizing metamorphosis
to let them clip your wings and
cage you.

my love, revenge isn't something you must seek…
for women like you, revenge is inevitably yours,
by simply
existing.

her strength was that she let
her pain
fuel her, not to seek revenge,
but to *rise*.

how authentic and beautiful
is a mind is that
cannot be bought;
a woman with ideas and beliefs
of her own,
unshaken by *anyone* or *anything.*

let them tell us that our heads are in
the clouds.

little do they know,
we the dreamers are the one's receiving
downloads from the heavens above,
and recoding the very world in which they live in.

maybe it's time to
refuse the chair at their table
and finally take off running wild
with the
wolves.

learn their traditions,
adapt to their instincts,
and allow their heat to warm
the blood inside of you
that has long been threatening
to run itself cold.

leave the others behind,
find your pack,
and hear them as they howl to you,
"welcome home."

CARTH ANGELS

somewhere beneath the anger,
beneath the scars,
and beneath the pain,
lies a place inside of my heart
where the old you still remains.

last night
i even met you there
to hear you asking me to stay…

i smiled and offered forgiveness,
and finally turned to walk away.

to my children:

one day you will learn
that magic is as real as the skin
on your body and the blood coursing
through your veins...

but my greatest hope for you,
soon after, is that you learn that the most
powerful and most beautiful magic of all time,
the only magic that will ever truly matter...

is to choose kindness in a world
that is tempting you to hate.

EARTH ANGELS

though her stride is of air
and of grace,
and though her spirit is of light,
never underestimate a woman that
transforms with the fall of
night.

when i weep
collect my tears and pour
them from off of the mountain tops…
let them be life giving to the flowers below
that are in need.

when i fall
may i be a stepping stone for someone
approaching the very same path.

when i am burning in the flames of
excruciating pain,
may my flames warm the soul of another.

and may i never get too comfortable
to lose this giving heart…

for without it, i am nothing.

i refuse to take offense to your
words rooted in jealousy...

for i too was once just like you —
a beautiful void
existing of eyelashes
and poisonous lips,
and i too could have almost any
man with the swing of my hips.

oh but life happened you see, and
fate chillingly showed up at my door
to finally tell me that i was born for
so much more.

so here i am, there you are,
and i recognize that our journeys look
quite the same...

therefore, i'll send you my love, wish you the
best, and pray that your heart soon finds it's way.

you were born for this —
all of this.
to fire-walk; to own the shadowed
valley; to emerge from the flames.

you only believed that you were weak,
but there is a monster raging on inside of you;
a fire that is all consuming.

they almost had you fooled though, right?
wrong.
they feared the day that you would wake
up to the truth… that you were created
defeatless, and forever you will remain strong.

she used the stars of her darkest night
to connect the dots,
brush herself off,
and rise again.

she said,
"i wont be caught once more losing myself
to the lies of weak spirited men."

blacked out,
i begin my ascension into the sky —

here to save the captives,

still dreaming of a forever,
you and i.

off slipped the clothing of her spirit,
and there loosened the grip of a bondage
that had long been tied.

one day you will awaken
and learn that you are the legend
of sleeping beauty;
the universe's queen.

and in the midst of the dream called
life,
you were being held in the arms
of your king.

how unfortunate it is that many
of us are stars,
plucked eagerly by hands
unequipped to handle our blazing
heat and our fiery light.

many of us then left completely
shattered, gathering the pieces
as we feel our way through the night.

others, at the very least,
left with gaping holes and a significantly
dimmer light.

and all of us sharing in common
homesickness and our desired
return to our places amidst the sky.

and how much more unfortunate it is
that of all the hands that we wish to be pieced
back together by, it is often times by the
very ones that plucked us from our homes,
carelessly leaving us to die.

and if you must walk this earth alone,
walk with courage,
and as if the guidance of a thousand
angels is before you.

because *they are*,
and because they a*lways have been*.

she is all things.
ubiquitous. present.
gentle.
salacious — dripping
unapologetically with
sensuality.

feral,
yet in the right moments,
tamed.

she is a constant evolution
of body mind, and soul;
an ethereal, never-ending
creation.

it may still be painful, yes…
because though you are now fire,
you are still learning to merge
with the elements around you.

with the air, you shall learn to
dance, careful to never break.
with the water, you shall learn to warm
it, careful not to let it put you out.
and with the earth,
you shall illuminate and ignite it,
careful not to make ashes of it.

your transformation is no doubt
beautiful, but with growth, you must
know always comes pain.

EARTH ANGELS

there truly is a land free flowing
with the purest of milk and the
sweetest of honey...

i danced there today
as i manifested love,
waltzing away from my former
self once and for all.

the secret to happiness is to stop
competing with the illusion of them;
stop competing with people that
have yet to walk through hell.

people who's talk is large,
yet experience small.

sheltered people, unaware that
at any given moment
they could be dealt the very cards as you.

people that would have folded the
hand that you have learned to play so craftily.

the one's that are able to thank their pain
for the lessons
and then gracefully release it...

those are the ones to be feared the most.

from my mind,
the weakness flees;

from my body,
the blood all dries...

and as every drop of
sweat hits the ground,
more of who i truly am is
recovered.

once lost...

but through the trials,
i am found.

these days i happen to value
my time alone…

for it is here that my soul is free to dream,
my mind free to travel,
and my heart free to love whom
it truly loves.

i noticed that the same one's that were
chastising me were licking honey
from their silver spoons
as i was making do with pulling scraps
from a dull knife…
a dull knife that i
had no other choice but to forge
my own path to hunt with.

they were overfed — senses so fixated on
their bellies that they ignored their hearts.

and how ironic, i then thought…
the entitled trying to convince the hunter
that she was weak.

.

EARTH ANGELS

they will kick you down in hopes of
dragging you to their height...
but to their dismay, they will find that
even at your worst, you still trump them
at their best.

if my home is here on earth,
then why is it that i begin to teleport
the moment the rays of the sun align
with my gaze?

if this is where i truly belong,
then why is it that the sky holds
the lyrics to my soul's favorited song?

is it too absurd to believe that i have blades
inserted into shoulders
where wings are meant to reside?
or that i have a body bound by gravity,
when my spirit was meant to fly?

CARTH ANGCLS

i have bled for you,
and i have bled for them...
never have i bled for myself.

too many times have i said
"yes" only to be taken advantage
of and abused;
too many times have i denied
myself, in the name of what was
"right"— in the name of you.

i am a woman tired of being taken from.
and though some may deem me 'faithless,'
i know myself to be the opposite now —
faith-filled,
focused,
and strong willed.

for the others
i will return...
but first,
i must save myself.

smiling,
i have watched another woman
hold the hand of the only one that
i whole-heartedly wished to keep.

smiling,
i have watched the world spin
around me,
while i remained frozen; stagnant.

smiling,
i have watched others capture their
dreams while i sang mine a lullaby
and rocked them all to sleep.

well,
gone is that smile for now,
and in place are eyes burning
with a pain driven focus.

the next smile i am to find
will be mine to forever keep…
birthed from the decision
to give to others,
but first, to give to me.

the voices will have no other choice
but to stop when they are overpowered
by your own...

be still, and *know.*

rise.

though we are the fallen
a n g e l s —
the outcasts to society…
we mustn't forget that
nothing here is as it seems.

'fallen,' just another word
for 'chosen,'

and chosen,
we will forever be.

so rise,
fallen a n g e l.
stand up and show the world your
unwavering strength.

EARTH ANGELS

heaven would love to have you,
my dear…

it's just…
well, it's complicated…
how do i put this?

right now, hell needs you more.

as i was rising i took a quick glimpse below
to find you silently choking on the wind beneath my
wings. i motioned for you, not just once but twice.
what i needed was for you to know that i never
wished this of you, and
that i had already made my plans to come back for
you, after having mastered the art of flight.

but blinded by your swiftness to see me fall,
you grabbed my every minuscule short-coming,
and you amplified them. you highlighted yourself
and did your best to cast shadows upon
my face; served me condescending words,
masquerading as a choice meal, concealed in
your falsity to care.

but i guess that's just the difference in you and i.
my tactic is to rise, and to pull others up with me.
and yours, to pull others down, more than likely
for the appearance of a rise —
a rise you are unwilling to put the blood, sweat,
and tears into.

from a shack to a castle,
this will be you.
but first, my love,
you must fearlessly let go
of everything that you once knew.

i will knock relentlessly
until the door opens.

the way i see it,
better bloody knuckles
than a broken soul.

to spit fire into fire,
what a disservice to one's own soul.

may i be known as water to the world
around me.

for as water, i am cut by the rocks,
all the while
knowing no pain.

as water,
i am a constant,
ever ebbing and flowing,
traveling my own course with ease.

and most importantly,
as water,
i am the element
that diffuses the fire.

in my life as a human
i am most certain i would have fallen
for you, and your lies,
as i fell for everyone and everything
else.

but you see,
a n g e l ' s, we don't fall...
we gracefully land.

if he caught a glimpse
of your wings
yet convinced you to land…

that wasn't love.

you know what's so fascinating about you?

higher powers have placed an inconceivable
amount of pressure upon you.

yet still with each time that you break,
you come back stronger than ever before.

the fairytales have us witches
all wrong…
we are not out here stirring blood,
or binding other human beings.

we're simply making magic out
of every day, ordinary things.

CARTH ANGELS

and even if you must release them
with shaking hands, a knot in your throat,
and trembling at the knees,

you must.

for soon after, you are free.

to the woman that he left behind:

i know that there's not a day that goes by
that you don't overanalyze yourself,
whether it be in the mirror,
or running internal errors of yourself
tirelessly through your mind.

i know that some days the thoughts of
him with her are enough to carry you
from an already cold and calculating day,
straight
into a sleepless night, with inescapable
nightmares.

and i know what it's like to fall
without much control, landing hellishly
on your now bruised and aching knees...
only it's not falling to pray, but falling to
mirror physically what you are already feeling
internally.

i know it's countless self-talks, what feels like
wasteful affirmations, and hours of training your
mind to obey your command to let them go.

it's a foreign world. a new reality.
when all you ever hoped for was a love that felt soft and
safe.

i know you, because i was you,
and i am also future you.

listen, you are not less than —
their capacity was.
and you are no second place or an abandoned home.

in time, you will see, that you were not being
punished, but spared, and that you are far from unloved,
but rather loved so much that god decided
you to be worthy of something more.

her kind of magic does not appear
in your life to simply up and vanish without
a trace.

it is inscribed into your heart
with eternal ink,
and synchronized into every detail of your life,
from there on after.

there is no escaping it once it finds you,
nor the desire to.

once her kind of magic touches you,
it forever lives inside of you.

EARTH ANGELS

be the rose that acknowledges
and gives thanks to the soil.

and may you find in this
not weakness,
but raw beauty and strength.

because remember,
nothing in this life
truly blooms without the help of
something
or someone else.

you are a beautiful array
of colors and hues,
bursting from the inside out.

and sure, you're a bit messy...
but isn't that the beauty of being
art?

just remember this,
a masterpiece should never
wish itself to change.

and if we are to weep,
let us weep with one eye
on hope
and the other on love…
for though trouble may
find us today,
it is ultimately to each and every
new morning
that our future belongs.

the sad truth is that we are all just wounded
children forced to play brave in adult
bodies.

CARTH ANGELS

if there is a spirit of a warrior to be found
in a woman,
i imagine a cut to the heart and a ripped seam
in the soul to be the necessary openings
from which it must first emerge.

if you're going to continue to drench others in grace,
it's time you stop condemning yourself as judas.

some of your greatest
strengths are weaknesses of
others,
but some of their greatest
strengths are noticeable
weaknesses of yours.

stay humble…
it's nothing to be ashamed of,
it's wisdom.

in this skin
i have both loved and i've lied;
been both the giver of life and
the destroyer of souls.

i know what it's like to be led
by flesh and too what it's like to
be led by the heart.

at best
i would say that i am a pendulum,
knowing my future but awaiting my
own steady and forgiving halt.

to myself, i beg of you, please slow down,
so that i can finally get to know you.

EARTH ANGELS

as far as the details of my future,
i haven't a clue.

but i know that in the grand scheme
of things
if you have yet to acknowledge my worth
then at least i will have...

and i will have departed from you,
once and for all,
bravely;
freely;
gracefully.

i used to think that i needed you
to see my worth; to desire me as
a moth flying into a flame.
i used think, if only i could be that
flame — the flame that you were
entirely consumed by;
the fire you were unafraid of;
the fire you would risk it all for.

i used to think.

well, i don't think anymore. i guess somewhere
along the way i grew tired of thinking.
i wanted to *feel.* i wanted to feel the opposite
of the way that you made me feel.
i was ready to feel worthy.

i used to think, but now, *i feel.*

i have in the same sentence both cursed
you and thanked you for leaving me.
i have been swallowed whole by the agony,
only to be spit out into the sky, amongst the stars,
floating weightlessly.

i am bound,
but above all, i am free.

because though i lost you,
i am slowly finding me.

EARTH ANGELS

more impressive than a natural
born heir of a thrown,
she was crowned queen
having survived the trials
and emerging from the flames.

what you are chasing, you already are.

a fire chasing another's flame…
why?

listen, if they wish to merge with you,
then effortlessly it shall be.

but if not,
it's time you re-stoke yourself,
and admire your own rising
flames.

imagine being an angel
so desiring of a specific fallen
that you were on the verge of clipping
your very own wings.

tell me, what service is it of,
to lower yourself,
and to fall alongside them?

as tempting as it may be,
you must remember your purpose
in the sky…
for it is only through you
that the two of you,
one day,
may have the opportunity to both fly.

stand strong,
hold onto your values,
and inspire him instead to rise.

EARTH ANGELS

in times that you feel as though
this is it for you, remember this…
you are an ellipsis.

at your worst you are merely a pause,
anticipating the continuation of the story…

but no where does your story truly end.

they are scissors with their words
because they felt uncomfortable
with your height.

the only tactic they know is to cut,
because they have yet themselves
learned to rise.

you are a
treasure worth seeking,
not something easily
found, nor possessed,
by hands so lazy and
ungrateful.

your body is a temple;
your mind, a portal;
your heart, valuable;
everything about you, *sacred*.
remember that the next time
you think to hand yourself over
so easily.

baby step your way into the kingdom
if you must.

first, exist until you live,
then live until you thrive,
and then thrive until you become a power
so undeniable
that they refer to you as a god.

EARTH ANGELS

the very hands that created the
cosmos,
the galaxy,
the oceans,
and the glistening of the sun,
created you.

you are more than beautiful…
you are a creation beyond your current
comprehension.

i shouldn't be here.
i shouldn't be fighting so hard to love myself
to make up for the lack of you not loving me.

sometimes playing with fire
and getting burned is necessary.

one moment you find yourself
lying on the floor as ashes,
and the very next,
you are remolding yourself
piece by piece,
coming out of the fire more
perfectly sculpted than ever before.

sometimes playing with fire burns you
into mere nothingness so that you are
forced to become something more.

and now i know the truth…
that you would have taken every healthy cell
in my body and coated it in disease, had i
let you.
you would have crushed me
as grapes in a winepress,
drinking every drop of me;
continued to diminish my light and
oppress my soul,
had i let you…
had i not finally learned to let you go.

if you have rendezvoused with fire,
consider yourself not cursed, but *chosen*.

for none come quite alive as those
touched by the flames.

it's hard to frighten a woman
like her
with your simple rain storms,
you know?

she once gave her everything to a hurricane.
he took her love, ran off, and destroyed her.
yet even in pieces, she found a way to
restore herself.

to be humble is not to deny yourself.
to be humble is to simply be aware that
the same greatness that lives inside of you
is available and ready to be accessed by
every other soul existing in this universe.

so the next time you think to water yourself
down,
try instead adding flavor to someone else.

when it hits you,
and it will hit you,
that i am no longer
in the world that we created
together,
there will still be a way to find me.

but i must warn,
small is the gate,
and narrow is the path;
hard to find,
and even harder to keep.
i couldn't stay this time,
even if i wanted to.
unless you learned, once
and for all, to cherish me.

allowing you to live inside of my mind
was fun while it lasted.

but allowing you to do so was as if i were
saying i was not worthy of having you in
all forms — body, mind, heart and soul.

goodbye, for now.

you came into my life as a hurricane,
and i shall leave yours as the faintest
whisper —
at first, unnoticed,
yet leaving behind a code that you will soon
beg to
transcribe.

i am not, nor was i ever
a woman to easily be forgotten.

i was and i still am
a woman worthy of not just a fraction,
but every fragment of your love.

i used to exist to please you.
my every inhale,
an attempt to breathe you
back in.

i found myself inhaling more
than i was exhaling.
i found myself deprived of
clean and new oxygen,
as i refused to release
the you that i had once breathed in.

but finally,
my breathing is again rhythmic;
finally i am balanced,
and i am healing.

and finally,
i am existing for myself, first,
and foremost…
and then for those, and only those,
that wish
to breathe in synchrony
alongside me.

this time
it's your turn to fight.
even winded,
in agony,
and through all of life's
dark and unknown paths.

now or never;
right here;
right now.

if you wish for me,
there is no need to run
after me,
but alongside me.

but no longer will i
run after someone,
running in the opposite
direction,
aware of my depleting breaths.

EARTH ANGELS

she withstands all storms,
and ultimately, she herself becomes them.

you tore me down as if i were in
need of a renovation. and for a moment in time,
i was trusting in you…believing in the remodel that
you had envisioned; allowing your hands amongst me,
the clay.

but when you left me there to put my own self
back together,
i lost so much respect for you.
you thought to make me into a soldier;
to strengthen me; to provoke me to rise…
when all i ever needed was your patience, your love,
and the two of us together, experiencing life.

i was in need of a remodeling,
not a full blown renovation.
i wanted to love, not to fight.

i said yes to please you.

i said yes again to please you further.

i said yes to please someone that i,
for the life of me, can't understand why
i would wish to please.

i said yes to you until my yes's felt
diseased.
i said yes until i could barely recognize me.

and though i am nearly unrecognizable,
at this point,
i am finally standing up and saying....

NO to you...
and yes,
to me.

solitude will always taste sweeter
when the bite before was saturated
in artificial flavoring to mask the taste of the
bitter, nutritionally void, fake company,
that you once craved.

sometimes i felt so drained by you that i failed
to remember who i was and who you were.

i am the hungry wolf, climbing the mountain.
you, nothing more than the tick on my skin,
free- loading on my blood.

the truth is,
i think little of you;
i focus on my own goals,
my own moves, and my own life.

but you,
so very weak and small,
you need me —
to live on;
to feed your emptiness;
to survive.

once the castle is built,
and the table has been set,
know that i am wishing
you a castle of your very
own...

but under no circumstances
may you continue to sit with me.

the hell you knowingly put
me through shed light on the
fact that you and i,
we are of different
kingdoms,
and quite honestly,
of very different worlds.

angels do not walk alongside snakes,
choosing cheap company as a means
to have any
at all.

angels choose solitude,
look deep inside,
and are believing of better company
to arrive in their future.

revenge is that first time you look at yourself
in the mirror with both a smile, and tear filled-eyes;
that moment you finally pulled through for
yourself.
it is the arrival to every occasion you rise to,
that they said could never be met.
it is the accomplishment of that very thing that
they fought so hard to keep you from reaching.
it is the phoenix that is birthed from their
pyromaniac tendencies; the healing that
miraculously takes place from the poisonous
seeds that they meant for harm.
it is every breath that you take apart from them;
every one of your dreams coming true;
everything that you do.

you.

you, yourself, you are the revenge.

of course you feel out of place...
you are star-seed, introducing heaven to earth.

CARTH ANGELS

you are something more than them...
and not because they are less fortunate,
or you are higher,
but because they chose their path,
as you have chosen yours.

if they wish to join you,
then so it shall be.
but if not, it is not your job to clip
your wings and walk alongside them.

you were created to inspire the rising
in others, not to lower yourself,
encouraging stagnancy.

EARTH ANGELS

some days it's going to feel as if
you are walking a balance beam —
heaven on one side, hell on the other;
revenge and forgiveness
both making their weight known
on the scales.

and on the these days,
i pray you find the strength to choose
forgiveness, because no offense is worth the
forfeiting of your soul.

you almost had the veil
completely over my eyes;
on the brink of choking on
and swallowing
your lies —
that you were worthy,
and that i was not;
that you were more and that
i was less.

i nearly died, chewing on your
own brokenness.

your bruises are beautiful,
you know?
they tell stories.
they're proof of your resiliency.
they're reminders of everything
that you have survived.

stop comparing yourself to
untouched skin.
you now have a beauty of your
own —
a breath-taking, chaotic, resilient,
beauty of your own.

\

it is said that a table will be
prepared for you,
in front of your enemies.

but i have reason to believe
that it will be taken a step further,
having them watch as you are
served a seven course meal.

stop saying that you will come out of this okay.

just okay is not enough. just okay is not what you deserve,
nor what you should wish to become.

think larger and speak mountains.

you are coming out of this taming fire,
and ceasing winds;
holding the universe,
and living out every last dream of yours.

you are coming out of this,
nothing short of thriving.

the next time someone tells you that a dream
or a desire of yours can not be obtained,

tell them the truth... *it is your birthright.*

fortunate are the mouths that
are fed freely.

but fortunate too are the mouths
that have learned endurance, wisdom,
and the art of hunting,
with sunken in ribs...

for they now are able to not only retrieve
for themselves, but to feed the mouths of others.

EARTH ANGELS

not all angels are created
the same.
some are created to instill balance,
some to soften hearts,
and others to seek justice.

and i think that willingness is the
prerequisite, roaming earth in human skin,
the test, and authenticity, the grade.

who will you become?

and if i must carry the weight
of your reckless abandonment within
my bones,

let it at least
keep me so heavily weighed down,
that i refuse to ever again chase you.

maybe i believed in you a little too much.
maybe i let your potential stand in front of your
actions, hiding them to the point
of an optical illusion.

as far as i was concerned, your poor actions
didn't so much as exist. who you were born to be —
who i knew you would grow into one day,
it's all i could ever see.
the best of you — it's all i'll ever see.

but now i know, that in order for you to reach that
potential, you must, *for now*, go on without me.

this will kill me,
walking away from the one
i swore i would never leave.

i can feel my breaths slowing,
and my heart's beat losing it's rhythm.
i sense the rattling approaching,
and my last breath nearing.

this will kill me,
i thought.

and then *you* finally stepped in
to save me.

i'm a fighter only because i had to be.
before the taunting, the abuse, and their
selfish use of their own free will,
i was love in it's purest form.

we all were.

and honestly, no matter how tough i
portray myself to be,
i long again to be
who i was before they programmed these
low vibrational codes into me.

i could let everyone that's ever
hurt me go and never to return again.
i could draw lines thicker than the ozone,
firm, and irreversible…
and i would be just fine.

but you?

why has letting you go always convinced me,
that soon after, i would die?

CARTH ANGCLS

i wish you could have loved
my chaos the way that i loved yours.
i wish you would have stayed.
i wish you had more patience.
i wish you had a larger capacity
to love.
i wish you could have seen yourself
with me.
i wish.
i wish.
i wish…

i wish honestly that i could just let you
go.

at the end of each and every day,
if you can lie your head down and
know that you gave it your absolute all,
even if you failed…
that alone is something to be proud of
and should assure you the sweetest rest.

now i'm breathing fast
to distract myself from reality.
i'm rocking back and forth
to still the thoughts of you and i.
i'm placing my feet firmly into
mother earth,
wishing that this was not required of me;
wishing that i didn't once and for all
have to let you go.

putting half of myself into
a balloon and releasing it into the sky;
further and further, i fade —
out of sight, yet painfully enough,
not out of mind…

this is what it feels like to release you.
for i am you, and you, i.

EARTH ANGELS

marked.

pursued.

loved.

forgiven.

—— *what you are to me.*

i finally left, but know that it was not up to me.
my self- worth stepped in and made
the call for me;
my heart stepped in to protect me;
my tears formed a river and my walls
a dam;

though i wished to,
i could no longer run back to you.

i clinched my fists,
tightened my jaw,
and closed my eyes,
to fight back the tears.

i gave it my all.

this is the part of the story
that i feared one day having to
write.

me finally letting you go;
me choosing me;
my rise.

an ending you would think would
be worthy of celebration,
but an ending that has me
feeling only half alive.

all of the chaos awakened the hurricane
that was merely at slumber inside of me.
it did not create me. it *asked of me* to show my face.

for i have always been raging winds,
piercing rain,
thunderous screams and lightning like
revenge;
a silent but deadly
sleeper,
waiting to take hold of everything
once stolen from me.

quitting you is just like quitting
any other drug, i would assume;
a grueling battle for sobriety.

it's learning to balance the serotonin
inside of my head, and saying no to
the increased and synthetic surges,
that you could promise me. it's waking
up every day, ready for battle; to say no,
and to choose the higher road — all of which
i am okay with…

but what i can't seem to come to terms with,
is that loving you was killing me, yet i had
never felt more alive, and that leaving you,
is restoring me… but ironically enough,
i feel half dead, afraid i will never survive.

when i walk through hell,
there are pictures frames
shattered on the floor;
the photos inside ripped
of you and i.
the voices taunt me,
"it's time to say goodbye."

in the main corridor,
the rug is ripped from underneath
my feet; and my blood, this time,
tastes far from sweet.
it is bitter; true to taste,
and the question is posed,
do i stay or do i
make haste?

hell is here —
being faced with this decision.
to choose you, or myself.

when all i ever wanted was
to choose us both.

EARTH ANGELS

no one ever tells you that the rising feels a lot like death,
but i will. i won't let another soul begin
ascension with false hopes and beliefs.
i want others to know what i wish i would have known.

and that is that flying feels a long like falling at first.
breathing feels unnatural.
letting go feels like losing all control.
choosing yourself feels foreign.
you look around and rarely do you feel at home.
even rest will begin to feel like work.
you'll fight. you'll fail. you'll push.
you'll climb. *you'll war...*

until the flying finally feels like ascension.
until the breathing is natural again.
until letting go, you learn, is to actually be in control.
until choosing yourself is the only thing that makes sense.
until you don't have to look around, you just
know that you're home.
until rest is felt, even while working.
until you fight and you achieve. until there
is no more pushing, no more climbing.

until you rise;
until you are free.

you're kicked down, you're not defeated,
and you're tired, you're not dead.

rest and try again....
you have all of the time in the world
to find your strength.

if the world were more kind,
i wouldn't have had to teach
myself to fly...

you would have taught me to —
your hand wrapped tightly
in mine.

from now on,
if you are to love me,
love me fervently;
if you are to pursue me,
pursue me relentlessly;
and if you are to know me,
you must study me tirelessly…

for anything short of this,
you may not have me.

remember, any woman targeted so heavily
must have something valuable beyond words
inside of her; something so powerful;
something in all actuality,
could never be taken from her.

"Humans become angels on earth,
not in heaven."

- Paramahansa Yogananda

Dedication:

To Jesus, the one that lives inside of me, believes in me, and walks through fire with me; the one that has promised to never forsake me. I will follow you, trust you, and love you, to the ends of this earth, and beyond, always and forever.

To my two children, Bradley & Noah. The times that the two of you have saved me from my own self and from the trials of this world have been far too many to count. You are mommy's tiny earth angels. Thank you for being my motivation and for being physical forms of the grace that I have for so long heard of.

To my parents and to my big brother, Derrick. Thank you for choosing me no matter what, in all of my many seasons. Thank you for your love, support and friendship, and for giving me a place called home.

AP, for believing in my dreams and encouraging me to pursue them; For helping to make pursuing them easier for me, by your constant love and support.

To my readers, thank you for finding value in my work. Each and every sale that I make is more than a sale to me, but a reminder that I am not alone in my feelings, my struggles, and my journey. These books aren't just mine, but ours.

with all of my love,

melissa m combs

Printed in Great Britain
by Amazon

73003518R00129